Selling Products and Services

A pictorial guide

Malcolm H. B. McDonald
and Peter Morris

BUTTERWORTH
HEINEMANN

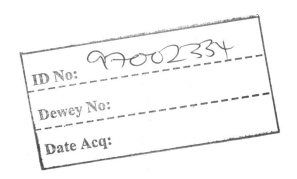

Butterworth-Heinemann Ltd
Linacre House, Jordan Hill, Oxford OX2 8DP

℞ A member of the Reed Elsevier group

OXFORD   LONDON   BOSTON
MUNICH   NEW DELHI   SINGAPORE   SYDNEY
TOKYO   TORONTO   WELLINGTON

First published 1991
Reprinted 1994

© Malcolm H. B. McDonald and Peter Morris 1991

British Library Cataloguing in Publication Data
A CIP catalogue record for this book is available from the British Library.

ISBN 0 7506 0069 1

Printed and bound in Great Britain

Selling Products and Services

Other books by Malcolm McDonald

How to Sell a Service: guidelines for effective selling in a service business
International Marketing Digest (co-edited with S. Tamer Cavusgil)
The Marketing Audit
Marketing by Matrix
The Marketing Plan: a pictorial guide for managers
The Marketing Planner
Marketing Plans: how to prepare them, how to use them
Retail Marketing Plans

Authors' Note

Butterworth Heinemann's Pictorial Guides are cartoon books with serious messages. This is our second Pictorial Guide. The first was called 'The Marketing Plan', and its success has encouraged us to explore the world of commercial transactions — selling products and services.

The six chapters follow the course of the sales process: from understanding the customers' needs, through getting an appointment to meet them, to the moment when the sale is closed. There's an introduction which examines the differences between selling services and products. At the end of each chapter there is an exercise to consolidate what has gone before. The primary purpose of this book is therefore to help sales staff new to the job and to remind the experienced manager of the steps on the way to sales success.

However, everybody constantly makes transactions of one kind or another, so the selling process embodies a fundamental human activity — the need to persuade somebody about something, so that both parties benefit. This is why we believe that this book could be read with profit, not only by sales executives, but by everyone.

Malcolm H.B. McDonald
Peter Morris

March 1991

Contents

Introduction

EVERYBODY SELLS...

MY GOLDFISH FOR YOUR ROD.

Everyone is involved in transactions.

Children are always exchanging things, and we all go on transacting throughout our lives.

IF I GOT A PROPER JOB, GLADYS, WOULD YOU MARRY ME?

I WOULD, CEDRIC.

Everyone has CUSTOMERS:

HE'S MINE

SHE'S MINE

HE'S MINE

HE'S MINE!

The success of the work we do depends on the co-operation of our colleagues. We are somebody's customer — and somebody else is ours.

Every person who SELLS also has to BUY...

SALESMAN.

BUYER.

Both the 'salesman' and his 'buyer' could be any of us, male or female, young or old...

... and whether we sell — or buy — services or products the **principle is the same.**

BUT...

1

Well, for a start, a service is not something you can see or touch. It isn't even **there** until it has been bought.

After all, with a **product** you know where you are. The customer can see what he's getting before he parts with his money.

But with a **service** ...

... you are asking a new customer to leap into the unknown.

From the customer's point of view, buying a service is like buying a **made to measure suit**.

You don't know what you are getting in advance.

2

Buying a product is like buying a ready-to-wear suit. You see what you are getting in advance.

And you know what the salesman's role is.

He's there to sell you the suit.

BUT... with the seller of a service it's different.

For instance, when somebody employs an architect, what does he think the end product will be?

Does the architect supply a house — or a drawing of the house? Is the customer buying the architect's expertise or the end-product?

Plans of 'DUNROAMIN'

YOU'RE QUITE RIGHT! IT SEEMS TO HAVE BROKEN DOWN.

I'LL HAVE A WORD WITH PRODUCTION.

A product salesman is not as much a part of what he's selling as a salesman selling a service is.

He can establish a relationship with his customer which to some extent can allow him to overcome weaknesses in the product.

Whereas in the case of the service salesman...

Report

...he himself is a much greater part of what he is selling.

I SAY...

This, plus the fact that the customer can't see what he's going to buy...

YOU'RE WEARING MY OLD SCHOOL TIE!

... makes him assess the salesman by some private, subjective set of criteria.

A SERVICE SALESMAN NEEDS TO BUILD TRUST AND A STRONG RELATIONSHIP WITH THE BUYER.

There's another difference between selling a service and selling a product...

QUICK! I NEED A TICKET FOR THIS AFTERNOON'S PLANE TO PARIS!

TERRIBLY SORRY — ALL SOLD... BUT I CAN DO YOU ONE ON YESTERDAY'S **HALF PRICE!**

... you can't **store a service!**

FINALLY: All products have a '**service**' element in them...

0% INTEREST ON HIRE PURCHASE

£ 7995 NEW

SALES

WHAT'S MORE, YOU GET AN UNCONDITIONAL FIVE YEAR RUST GUARANTEE AND A YEAR'S FREE SERVICING..

... and all services have a '**product**' element:

I SELL PHOTOCOPIERS

I SELL A PHOTOCOPYING SERVICE

WITH MY COPIERS COMES A COMPREHENSIVE **SERVICE**

...AND MY SERVICE INCLUDES **SUPPLYING** PHOTO-COPIERS.

...SO MY CUSTOMER GETS WHAT'S NEEDED — A **RELIABLE** PHOTOCOPYING SERVICE.

BUT, WHETHER YOU SELL PRODUCTS **OR** SERVICES, YOU'LL MEET THE **SAME** PROBLEMS ...

Problems
associated with selling Products and Services

RACHEL, FIND OUT WHO GIVES COURSES IN TELEPHONE TECHNIQUES, WILL YOU? WE NEED SOME STAFF TRAINING.

WHO, ME?

And, eventually...

MEGABIZ your local multinational

Mr. Smooth
Training Consultant

Dear Mr. Smooth,

It has been
recent revi
relation
is requ
Pleas

MEGA your local multina

Mr. Ruff
Training Consultant

Dear Mr. Ruff,

It has been decided foll
recent review of Pu
relations poli
is requi
Ple

... both salesmen were invited to discuss their services.

Here's what the Foolish Salesman did...

HELLO, SQUIRE!

He telephoned the man in Megabiz who had written to him.

I HAVE THE ANSWER TO **ALL** YOUR TRAINING PROBLEMS!

I'M YOUR MAN!

LEAVE IT **ALL** TO ME!

DON'T WORRY ABOUT A **THING**, MATEY!

ALL YOU HAVE TO DO IS **SIGN** THE **CHEQUE**!

HA! HA! HA!

6

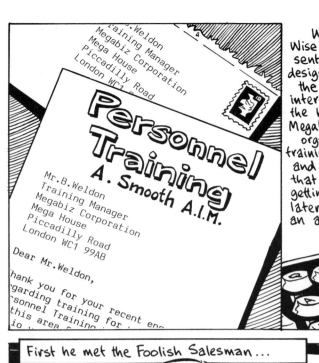

Personnel Training
A. Smooth A.I.M.

Mr.B.Weldon
Training Manager
Megabiz Corporation
Mega House
Piccadilly Road
London WC1 99AB

Dear Mr.Weldon,

Thank you for your recent enq
regarding training for
Personnel Training for
this area

Whereas the Wise Salesman sent a letter designed to capture the enquirer's interest, stressing the benefits to Megabiz of his organisation's training programmes and indicating that he would be getting in touch later to arrange an appointment.

In the event...

The Training Manager at Megabiz decided to meet both salesmen separately to hear their views and make comparisons.

First he met the Foolish Salesman...

HI, BRIAN!! HOW'S IT GOING SQUIRE?!

... who treated him like a long-lost friend.

...AND WE'LL CLOSE THE WHOLE PLACE DOWN FOR A WEEK AND TRAIN 'EM ALL AT ONCE...

...GET 'EM AWAY FROM THE PLACE... PUT 'EM UP AT A DECENT HOTEL...

?

The Foolish Salesman had plenty to say for himself, especially as he hadn't heard what his prospective client had to say yet...

The Training Manager had done some homework before the salesmen were due to arrive.
He had talked to some of his colleagues at Megabiz and assessed the problem...

WHILE WE'RE LOOKING AT THE RECEPTIONISTS' TRAINING WE MIGHT THINK OF OTHER AREAS...

SOME OF THE FOLK IN THE SERVICE DEPARTMENT KEEP CUSTOMERS WAITING FAR TOO LONG.

THE LADS ON THE PRODUCTION LINE FIGURE THEY DON'T NEED TO KNOW WHAT THE REST OF THE FIRM DOES...

HMM... WE'VE BEEN A BIT LAX ALL ROUND ABOUT CUSTOMER RELATIONS...

All his consultations with his colleagues had convinced the Training Manager...

...SO, J.B, I THINK WE HAVE TO TAKE THIS TRAINING THING VERY SERIOUSLY INDEED. THE STAFF'S ATTITUDE IS LOSING US CUSTOMERS...

WE HAVE TO CALL SOMEBODY IN...

DO IT

8

So a NEW proposal can be a difficult one to sell...

... given the number of people who will have to be convinced.

... whereas if the salesman has done business with the company before a repeat order would need only the approval of the buyer.

HELLO ERIC, HOW'S THE WIFE?

HELLO SAM, NICE TO SEE YOU.

The size and make-up of the Decision-Making unit are affected by:

✳ The degree of **NEWNESS**

✳ **COST**

✳ **COMPLEXITY** of the sales proposal

The Wise Salesman also knew that even the obvious person – the Training Manager – wasn't necessarily the one making the important decisions on the transaction.

CONTRACT

Of course the Foolish Salesman was not troubled by complications like that

ARE YOU **MAN** OR **MOUSE?**

Had he put himself in the customer's position he might not have made some of the mistakes he did make.

To the customer the problem went something like this :

GO AWAY!

STAFF ARE RUDE...

TRAINING!

① Something is wrong

② Problem is identified

③ Solution is specified

④ Discussion takes place with all interested parties

This was where the Wise and Foolish Salesmen came in ...

HM.. THERE COULD BE A LOT OF TRAINING IN THIS FOR SOMEBODY...

BETTER MAKE SURE WHOEVER I GET CAN HANDLE ALL OF IT.

But what neither of them knew was exactly what the job entailed. The Wise Salesman was aware of this ...

JUST LEAVE IT TO **ME**, SQUIRE!

... but the Foolish Salesman was not.

WHAT DO YOU THINK?

ER.. I'LL HAVE TO CONSULT MY COLLEAGUES.

WHAT?!

WHO WEARS THE PANTS, DECISION-WISE, ROUND HERE?

What the Foolish Salesman hadn't realised – but the Wise Salesman had – was that a number of people in Megabiz were involved in the decision-making process.

Of course there was the Training Manager, who would want to know the details of the course.

But the Production Manager would also need to know how much time off would be needed for the workforce.

And the Finance Dept. would certainly want to know about the training budget.

Then, the Managing Director always took an interest in all new schemes.

WE NEED TO CHANGE STAFF ATTITUDES.

NOW LOOK HERE, BROTHER...

WHAT WILL IT MEAN FOR MY MEMBERS?

What's more, the Union representatives might need counselling, particularly if work patterns might be changed...

In his meeting with the Training Manager, the Wise Salesman would find out who the people involved were.

Each had his or her own point of view — but the Wise Salesman regarded them as a UNIT...

DECISION MAKING UNIT

... a unit in which the various requirements of the members must be taken into account, and in which any proposal suggested by the salesman would need to be presented in a different way to each of the individuals concerned.

HOW WILL IT AFFECT PRODUCTION?

HOW MUCH WILL IT COST?

HOW WILL IT AFFECT WORKING CONDITIONS?

WILL WE END UP MORE PROFITABLE?

WHAT WILL IT ACHIEVE?

A new proposal like this one would have to be spelled out to a number of interested parties in terms which would explain its effect on their sphere of influence.

5 Executive decision is taken to proceed

6 Search for supplier of the solution begins

7 Proposals received and evaluated.

8 Most appropriate one chosen.

9 Contract signed.

Finally, project is monitored, and, at the end, evaluated.

Now let's take a look at some of the points covered in this tale...

1. Credibility

The Wise Salesman established his credibility before speaking to the buyer.

Whereas the Foolish Salesman rushed right in with solutions before he knew what the problems were.

2. Behaviour

HOW DO YOU DO?

The Wise Salesman adopted a courteous manner towards his customer...

SPINELESS OR WHAT?!

... unlike the Foolish Salesman.

3. Awareness

And he was also aware that there are generally several people involved in the buying process, so he took their needs into account when making his proposal.

There are differences between selling to an organisation and selling to an individual ...

I SAY!! YOU'RE WEARING MY OLD SCHOOL TIE JOLLY GOOD... JOLLY GOOD!!

An individual buyer's subjective criteria might prove decisive in whether the seller gets the job.

In the case of an organisation the first impression a salesman might get is that he is dealing with a large number of people if the company is a large one...

WHAT DO YOU WANT?

... then the next impression might be that he is dealing with an individual ...

...'The Buyer.'

BUYER

BUYER

In practice, although the salesman comes face-to-face with one person who represents the interest of the buying company, that person will need the approval of others for any decision he or she may want to make.

The personal authority of the buyer is governed by three factors:

AH-HEM

COST
NEWNESS
COMPLEXITY

The more expensive a project is likely to be, or the more innovative, or the more it will involve larger numbers of people in its execution, the less it's going to be possible for one member of an organisation to make a decision on his own.

So the person with the title of BUYER...

TELL HIM...

DON'T FORGET TO MENTION...

MAKE SURE HE KNOWS ABOUT...

...is not necessarily the free agent we like to think he is.

There are generally several people or several groups of people in an organisation who are involved in the buying decision.

We call these people the Decision Making Unit, or DMU for short.

DMU

The Salesman must be able to identify the Decision Making Unit, which will enable him to see the transaction from the buyer's point of view, and help him provide a sales proposal in line with the customer's requirements.

THIS ONE

THIS ONE

THIS ONE

But as well as the DMU, there might be other influences working on the buyer...

ECONOMIC SITUATION BZZ... POLITICAL CONSIDERATIONS COMPETITION ENVIRONMENT BZZ BZZ...

Outside pressures from the business environment which could affect plans for investment...

BETWEEN THE TWO OF US...

I DON'T THINK THE OLD MAN WILL LIKE IT!

... and pressures from inside the company; such things as confused information, unwieldy organisation, rivalry, internal politics, and so on. A salesman has to detect these pressures and take account of them.

THE SALESMAN MUST RESEARCH HIS CUSTOMER'S NEEDS, ESPECIALLY IN THE CASE OF A NEW BUY.

PERHAPS

DON'T KNOW

MAYBE

With a New Buy the Salesman has to work hard. All decision makers have to be met and influenced.

It takes time.

But if the buyer merely wants to repeat his order — a straight re-buy — there is no such rigorous examination of the buy-phases.
Questions of price, standards and delivery deadlines are easily settled.

However, if there are significant differences between this and the original contract...

SAME AGAIN

... there will have to be a modified re-buy.

MODIFIED, EH? I'LL HAVE TO ASK.

WHAT WAS WRONG WITH..?

WE'LL HAVE TO COST IT OUT.

Some or all of the buy-phases will have to be re-examined, and the salesman may have to meet the members of the Decision Making Unit all over again.

BUT, this IS the advantage of a modified re-buy.

IT'S OLD WHATSISNAME AGAIN!

It tends to strengthen the salesman's relationship with members of the Decision Making Unit.

Exercise 1

IDENTIFYING THE DECISION-MAKING UNIT

An important reason for identifying the DMU for your product or service is to improve your sales efficiency. There is little point in spending your selling time with people who are not part of the DMU. You can even take the concept further by identifying the key individuals in the DMU and devoting most of your time and effort to them.

The worksheet on the next page is a Customer Analysis Form for a typical large customer. It allows you to identify the members of the DMU and what information each member might require.

How to Use the Customer Analysis Form

The form includes a list of possible members of a company's decision-making unit. Enter the name and title of each relevant member in one of the blank boxes along the top of the form. (If necessary change the names of the departments.) The form also contains a list of typical decision-forming factors which might be considered by different managers at various stages of the selling process. Other factors relevant to your product or service can be added. To use the matrix, indicate for each management function and each stage of the buying process in which they are likely to be involved, those factors each member of the DMU will take into account in arriving at a decision. Do they each have the appropriate information on your product? What is the most effective method of communicating this information to each manager?

1. If you sell to businesses, complete the form for your three major customers. Compare the analysis with what actually happens. Have you met all the members of the DMU? Do you supply all the information they need?

2. If you sell to individuals, construct a similar form identifying all the individuals in the DMU. You may wish to add further factors for consideration to the list. Compare the analysis with what actually happens. Have you met all the members of the DMU, or at least supplied them with the information they need, in the form in which they need it?

3. From your knowledge of the members of the DMU and their roles, identify which individuals have the major influence on the buying decision.

CUSTOMER ANALYSIS FORM

Customer's name & address	
Salesperson	Tel. no.
Products / Services	**By class:** New buy / Straight re-buy / Modified re-buy
Date of analysis	
Date of reviews	

Member of Decision-Making Unit (DMU)	Production	Sales & Marketing	Research & Development	Finance & Accounts	Purchasing	Data Processing	Other
Buy phase				*Enter name and title of individual in appropriate box below*			
1. Recognises need or problem and works out general solution.							
2. Works out characteristics and quantity of what is needed.							
3. Prepares detailed specification.							
4. Searches for and locates potential sources of supply.							
5. Analyses and evaluates tenders, plans, products.							
6. Selects supplier.							
7. Places order.							
8. Checks and tests product.							

Factors for consideration

1 price	2 performance	3 availability
4 back-up service	5 reliability of supplier	6 other users' experience
7 guarantees and warranties	8 payment terms, credit, or discount	9 other, e.g. past purchases, prestige, image, etc.

Adapted from J. Robinson, C.W. Farris, and Y. Wind, *Industrial Buying and Creative Marketing*, Allyn and Bacon, 1967.

Reaching the Customer

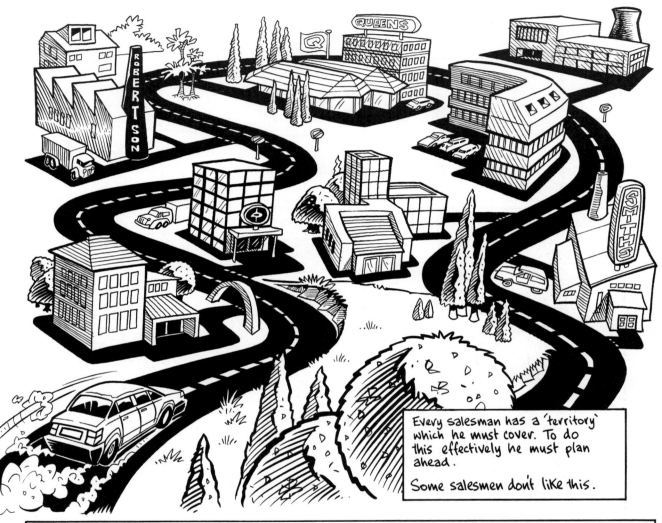

Every salesman has a 'territory' which he must cover. To do this effectively he must plan ahead.

Some salesmen don't like this.

To them it implies inflexibility, which will inhibit their ability to meet new circumstances.

They can see difficulties in dealing with sudden requests or complaints, problems in co-ordinating interviews, parking and so on.

WHAT'S MORE ... they think it leaves no opportunity to find new business!

NEW TERRITORY

BAH! NO TIME!

PLANNING AHEAD DOES NOT MEAN THIS.

THANKS!

Mon

Tues

PLENTY OF TIME!

What it does mean is that planning must be flexible enough to give the salesman ROOM TO MANOEUVRE — to give him time to cope with unforeseen circumstances and to be able to take new opportunities as they arise.

IN FACT, ONLY BY PLANNING HIS ACTIVITIES CAREFULLY WILL THE SALESMAN HAVE THE FREEDOM TO COPE WITH NEW CIRCUMSTANCES.

But too many salesmen find that they have too little time to keep up.

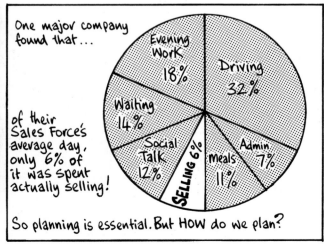

One major company found that...

of their Sales Force's average day, only 6% of it was spent actually selling!

Evening Work 18%

Driving 32%

Waiting 14%

Social Talk 12%

SELLING 6%

meals 11%

Admin 7%

So planning is essential. But HOW do we plan?

The first thing to do is to take a good look at your customers and **classify them.**

Is your relationship with them ...

CUP OF TEA, LUV?

Friendly?

BOOT!

Hostile?

WE..ER..HAD AN APPOINTMENT...

ZZZZZZZZZ

Indifferent?

And which of them are...

...and work out how often you should call on them.

BIG SPENDERS

MEDIUM SPENDERS

LOW SPENDERS

Estimate your workload.

Find out what you can reasonably expect to achieve in one day and allocate the number of calls you plan to make on that basis.

Now plan your territory in detail. It may take a few attempts before you get it right.

So here's a tip...

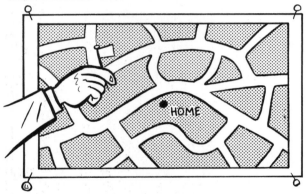

Place a large, transparent plastic sheet over the map and stick in coloured pins or flags showing your existing and potential customers.

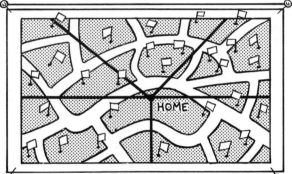

Now divide the territory into segments, one for every day of the working week, and plan your daily route in each segment.

The transparent sheet means you can rub out a route and try again if you get it wrong.

PLANNING A ROUTE.

Some salesmen start at the furthest point from home and work their way back.

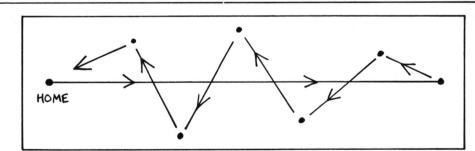

But a shorter solution might be this:

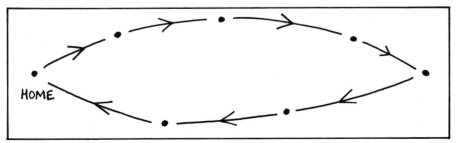

24

By selecting a route for each of the segments, the salesman is now able to make the best use of his time — and if he needs to make an unscheduled call in another segment, he is much better able to plan when he can do it.

That means he's somewhere near all his customers at least once a week — and when something unexpected crops up he can cope with it with the minimum expense or delay.

CLASSIFYING CUSTOMERS.

We saw earlier that customers can be classified into three groups of spenders...

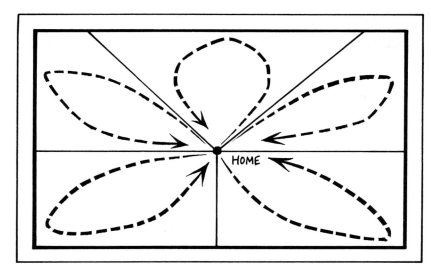

...and that they can be categorised as hostile, indifferent or friendly.

Make these two sets of characteristics into a grid...

	BIG	MEDIUM	LOW	
				FRIENDLY
				INDIFFERENT
				HOSTILE

CUSTOMERS' CHARACTERISTICS.

By plotting what kind of customer each company you deal with is, you will be able to plan your time more profitably and give yourself more opportunities for contacting customers with the most potential.

	BIG	MEDIUM	LOW
FRIENDLY	*	*	*
INDIFFERENT			
HOSTILE			

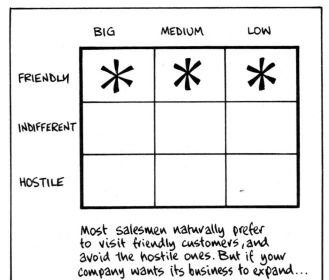

Most salesmen naturally prefer to visit friendly customers, and avoid the hostile ones. But if your company wants its business to expand...

	BIG	MEDIUM	LOW
FRIENDLY			
INDIFFERENT	*	*	
HOSTILE			

... you'll also need to visit the big and medium-sized companies who, so far, are indifferent to your company's products or services. Here lies the greatest potential for improved sales productivity.

	BIG	MEDIUM	LOW
FRIENDLY	*	*	
INDIFFERENT			
HOSTILE			

Meanwhile, it's important to maintain existing contacts with these big and medium-sized friendly companies...

	BIG	MEDIUM	LOW
FRIENDLY			
INDIFFERENT			
HOSTILE	*	*	

... while with these hostile customers it's going to be necessary for you to change your sales tactics.

	BIG	MEDIUM	LOW
FRIENDLY			*
INDIFFERENT			*
HOSTILE			

With friendly and indifferent customers amongst the low spenders you can afford to spend correspondingly less time...

	BIG	MEDIUM	LOW
FRIENDLY			
INDIFFERENT			
HOSTILE			*

... and with the hostile small spender, little or no time at all!

Of course there can be no definitive rule about the frequency of sales visits, but knowing your customers' characteristics helps find out if your time is being spent productively.

You've determined who you need to see, and you've planned your route.

You are now all set to meet your customer. How do you now go about getting that crucial interview?

COME IN! **BOY** HAVE I GOT AN ORDER FOR **YOU!**

With regular customers this is easy. But how do you get interviews with **potential** ones?

GETTING INTERVIEWS WITH NEW CLIENTS.

A new client company is unknown territory. You don't know who the Decision-Making Unit is, there are no personal relationships to start from and everyone is busy.

What's more, they are **protected**...

... by a screening system.

MR. SMITH IS IN CONFERENCE.

To get past the various barriers of receptionists, secretaries, personal assistants and so on, the salesman has to put a good case.

The first difficulty is in establishing contact.

Secretary.

Receptionist.

27

Even if you overcome the initial problem of establishing contact by telephone ...

SO IF YOU'RE NOT DOING ANYTHING, SQUIRE ...

... it may be even more difficult to make a proposition attractive enough to tempt the prospective customer to meet you.

On the other hand ...

HOW ABOUT IT?

SAVE

COME RIGHT OVER!

... most appointments are made over the telephone, on the initiative of the salesman.

So, how is it done?

① PREPARE THE WAY WITH A LETTER.

The letter of introduction to a prospective client should reflect the personality of the writer, so it's impossible to specify the words that should be written, but there are certain things it MUST contain.

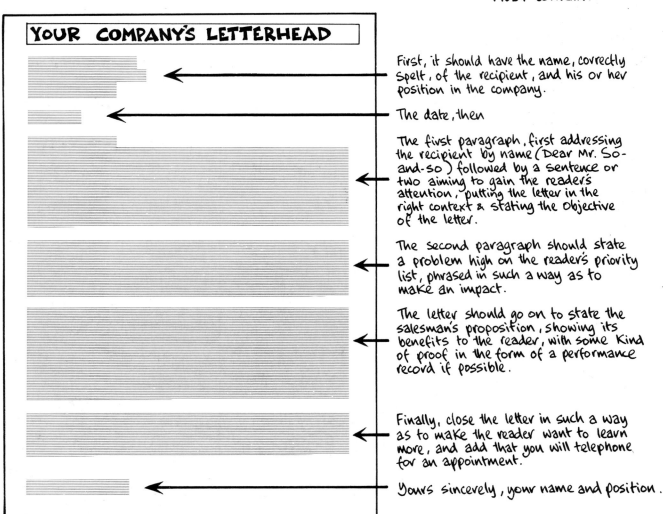

YOUR COMPANY'S LETTERHEAD

First, it should have the name, correctly spelt, of the recipient, and his or her position in the company.

The date, then

The first paragraph, first addressing the recipient by name (Dear Mr. So-and-so) followed by a sentence or two aiming to gain the reader's attention, putting the letter in the right context & stating the objective of the letter.

The second paragraph should state a problem high on the reader's priority list, phrased in such a way as to make an impact.

The letter should go on to state the salesman's proposition, showing its benefits to the reader, with some kind of proof in the form of a performance record if possible.

Finally, close the letter in such a way as to make the reader want to learn more, and add that you will telephone for an appointment.

Yours sincerely, your name and position.

Writing to your potential customer has advantages over other forms of written communication, like mail shots, because you are in direct contact with the person you want to see — and you have prepared the ground for your phone call.

GOOD MORNING, MR. SMITH!

Mr. Smith
Chief Buyer
Jinx & Co.

But, before you phone...

Diary

PREPARE

Your carefully worded letter will be a waste of time if you just pick up the phone and dial.

Phonecall checklist.

① Reserve an hour of your time each week just for phoning contacts.

② Make a list of people you want to call based on your territory.

③ Make sure you know what you want to get out of each call before you make it.

④ Keep a note of the questions and individual needs of each client.

⑤ Decide on your telephone manner for each call.

⑥ Make sure you can make appointments if the opportunity arises.

⑦ Work from a location where background noise will not distract you.

② MAKE CONTACT BY PHONE.

You've prepared the way with a letter of introduction and you have made sure that you have completed your phonecall checklist.

All you've got to do now is dial the number... but it's not going to be as easy as that.

When you dial, one of two things is likely to happen...

EITHER

The line is engaged. If so, pass on to the next customer on the list.

OR

The operator on the client's switchboard acts as a screen.

GO AWAY.

Here your letter of introduction comes in handy.

I WANT TO TALK TO MR. SMITH OR HIS SECRETARY MISS JONES ABOUT A LETTER.

Here you must sound spontaneous and authoritative. The likely result of this will be...

MR. SMITH'S OFFICE — CAN I HELP YOU?

Having arrived at the client's secretary, you can again quote the letter, perhaps in more detail, and address her by name if possible.

HELLO, IS THAT MISS JONES? JEFF WHEELER HERE FROM ABC...

Now you're in a position to state the purpose of your appointment and ask for help.

Remember, she will have read your letter and this will give you an advantage.

With ordinary luck you will now arrive at...

OH, HELLO MR. WHEELER. YES I REMEMBER. MR. SMITH HAS YOUR LETTER...

YES?

...your client!

Your call will have three phases:

THE OPENING THE LEVER THE CLOSE

IS THAT MR. SMITH?

SPEAKING.

The first thing to do is to make sure you are speaking to the right person.

Then introduce yourself, giving both your name and the name of your company.

JEFF WHEELER, ABC PRODUCTS!

UH-HUH!

Now make your LEVER statement.

DID YOU GET MY LETTER?

Refer to your letter or a previous call. State your common interest – the area you want to make an impact on.

YOU'RE RIGHT—IT'S A PROBLEM KEEPING SALES' OVERHEADS DOWN.

Once you have established this common interest you are ready to CLOSE the conversation.

You want to VISIT him.

The close should be as quick as possible.

WE DID A SIMILAR EXERCISE WITH XYZ AND THEY SAVED 20%

PERHAPS WE COULD TALK ABOUT YOUR SITUATION

WOULD MONDAY OR TUESDAY DO FOR YOU?

Of course, not all phone calls are as easy as this...

I'M A **BUSY MAN,** MR. WHEELER!

...So you may have to meet some objections.

There are two main types, and this is the first – the client is too busy to see you.

Resist the temptation to play down the objection.

HE THINKS **HE'S** BUSY! **HUH!** HE DOESN'T KNOW WHAT **BUSY** IS!

I do understand, Mr. Smith ... it's the busy people who get things done ... may I suggest that my scheme will ease the burden ...

Suggest for example that your product or service will benefit him by increasing his company's production efficiency, thus increasing its profitability. If he's still too busy to see you, suggest that you call him back at a more convenient time, or that you meet him very early or late in the day.

DO YOUR HOMEWORK.

I THINK I CAN DEMONSTRATE CONSIDERABLE SAVINGS TO YOUR COMPANY.

The promise of benefits to his business is an important ingredient in getting a buyer to see you, so make sure you will be able to keep your word.

This homework will go a long way to countering the second objection you may meet ...

DON'T NEED YOU ...

Particularly if the real reason for not wanting to see you is inertia.

..WE HAVE **BIGGS.**

BIGGS IS GOOD, MR. SMITH, BUT THIS MIGHT BE A GOOD OPPORTUNITY TO COMPARE COSTS.

But if the reason is that they already have a supplier, DON'T KNOCK THE OPPOSITION — it immediately reflects on your potential client's judgement —

AFTER ALL, THERE'S NO OBLIGATION ON YOUR PART ...

— but suggest that a meeting will at least give him a chance to compare your respective products or services.

OH, OK. WHAT HAVE I GOT TO LOSE?

There is now a very good chance that the buyer will agree to an appointment. Confirm the date and time by letter immediately.

THE APPOINTMENT.

Your appointment will have to be co-ordinated with others. If one runs late, telephone ahead to the next one or perhaps two, re-arranging the time until you get back on schedule.

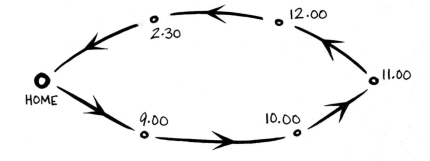

HOME
9.00
10.00
11.00
12.00
2.30

If your prospective client is very busy, he or she will not yet be under pressure if you arrange your appointment early.

Smith & Smith

CLOSED

milk

GLAD TO SEE YOU'RE AN EARLY BIRD TOO, MR. WHEELER!

In the same way, the pressure is likely to have eased off by late afternoon...

5:45 PM

THE ONLY TIME THE PHONE STOPS RINGING!

... and fewer salesmen from competing companies will want to see buyers on Monday mornings or Friday afternoons.

The same goes for lunchtimes.

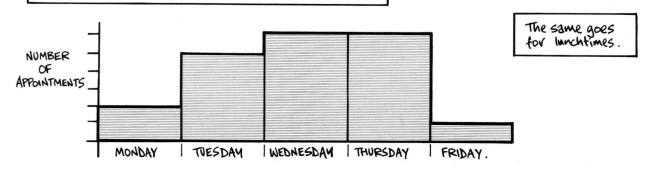

NUMBER OF APPOINTMENTS

MONDAY | TUESDAY | WEDNESDAY | THURSDAY | FRIDAY.

And don't forget – those members of the Decision Making Units who are on night shift are always easier to see.

THANK YOU FOR SEEING ME, MR. WILKINS.

LET'S MAKE IT FROM 4·40 TO 4·50 ON FRIDAY AFTERNOON THEN.

A last tip : a specific appointment which is neither on the hour or half hour reassures the buyer that you will keep your word when you ask for 'just ten minutes of his time'.

FINALLY, TO RECAP :

MEETING YOUR CUSTOMER

Determine worthwhile customers

Estimate realistic workload

Delineate territory

Reserve time for telephoning customers

Develop tactics for reaching them

Be creative and flexible in arranging appointments

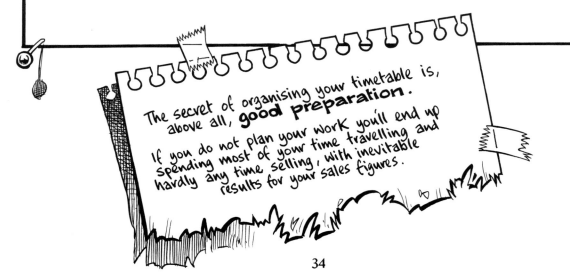

The secret of organising your timetable is, above all, **good preparation.**

If you do not plan your work you'll end up spending most of your time travelling and hardly any time selling, with inevitable results for your sales figures.

Exercise 2

WRITING A SALES LETTER

Many salesmen find that their ability to secure an interview over the telephone is increased if they precede their call with a letter. However, writing a sales letter is a skill which has to be learned. There may be a fortunate few who are 'naturals' when it comes to writing sales letters, but most of us are not. Take the example of the letter on the next page. The writer, Mr G.H. Bennett, is not an uneducated man and he is a very experienced bank manager. What do you think of his 'sales letter'?

Step 1	Write down all the points about this letter where you think improvements could be made.
Step 2	Compare your critique of the letter with the suggestions put forward in the Answer Section below.
Step 3	Observing all the 'rules' for improvements to a sales letter developed in Steps 1 and 2, write a sales letter to a potential customer of yours.
	Note: It is intended that you should be prepared to send the final version of your letter to an *actual* customer.
Step 4	After posting the letter, and allowing for delivery and reading time, telephone the customer with a view to making an appointment.

THE INTERNATIONAL BANK

Commercial Street
Ourtown
West Midlands
OT2 2LG

Our Ref: GHB/jf

The Managing Director
Acme Engineering Co Ltd
Britannia Industrial Estate
Ourtown
West Midlands

27 February 1991

Dear Sir

I have recently taken over the management of the Ourtown Branch of the International Bank and am endeavouring to make contact with as many representatives of local business as as possible.

I am not of course in possession of full details of your Company but feel sure there will be many areas in which we can be of assistance.

Many companies from time to time require finance and in addition to the normal facilities in this respect the bank's Business Development Loan Scheme provides assistance well suited for expansion plans which involve the purchase/extension of premises and/or the provision of new machinery. It may be of course that finance could be required, geared towards working capital and you may find details of the bank's factoring operations including invoice discounting of interest in this respect.

We do, of course, through our subsidiary, International Data Services, offer a full payroll service with the many benefits including cost savings this represents, together with a full accounting service and other ancillary computer based services.

Commercial insurance too is available through International Insurance Services Limited, one of the largest broking companies in the country and able therefore to bring to bear the full resources of the bank to offer the best all round package to fulfil all your company's insurance needs from vehicle cover to pension plans.

I have taken the opportunity of enclosing leaflets giving more details of the services I have mentioned, together with a full selection of material that gives an indication of the very wide financial package the bank can offer.

It would I am sure be of mutual benefit if we can meet and discuss ways in which we could assist and to this end I await your response when we may make the necessary arrangements.

Yours faithfully

G. H. Bennett
Manager

36

SUGGESTED ANSWERS

Having analysed Mr G.H. Bennett's letter to Acme Engineering Co. Ltd. you should have made some comments about the following points:

The Addressee   Is the Managing Director the person who will be most interested in the service? Might the Financial Director have been a more appropriate recipient? Always use the name of the recipient, even if you have to phone the company to check what it is.

Presentation   Nothing in the presentation makes it personal to Acme Engineering. It is obviously a printed 'Yours faithfully' circular and as a result doesn't command much attention.

Content   The letter has one or two things to commend it, for example

(a) it introduces several important items
(b) it has some customer appeal because the writer has personalized it by using the first person singular, e.g. 'I have taken over'. 'I have taken the opportunity', etc.

However, overall the letter is fairly dull and lacks punch. (Did it capture your interest?) There are too many weak phrases e.g. 'You may find details of the bank's factoring operations of interest', 'gives an indication', 'it would I am sure' .... The final phrase does not invite positive action and contains no lever for selling when the letter is followed up. The last paragraph is terribly stilted English and is a typical example of outdated business language.

Length   Since the letter was designed to arrange an appointment, it did not need to be as long or as complex as it was. One or two good reasons for a meeting would be enough.

On the next page is an example of the letter as it might have been written. You will note how reference to a newspaper story is quoted as a lever. (While this lever was 'invented', in your letter some form of lever should be included.)

THE INTERNATIONAL BANK

Commercial Street
Ourtown
West Midlands
OT2 2LG

Our Ref: GHB/jf

The Managing Director
Acme Engineering Co Ltd
Britannia Industrial Estate
Ourtown
West Midlands

27 February 1991

Dear Sir

I have recently taken over the management of the Ourtown Branch of the International Bank. It was my intention to make contact with you in the normal course of business, but having just read about Acme Engineering's success in winning its first export contract, it seemed more appropriate to do so now.

Sorting out the financial arrangements and coping with the mass of documentation and administration procedures can be something of a headache for first time exporters like yourselves.

But they don't have to be.

The International Bank has helped many companies like yours to become thriving exporters. When we combine our expert services with our client's natural business enterprise, it always proves to be a winning formula.

We really ought to meet and discuss the ways our services could save you time and effort and reduce the risks at this exciting stage of your company's development.

I will contact you early next week to check when a meeting would be most convenient.

Yours faithfully

G. H. Bennett
Manager

The Interview

If you have done your homework, found out the relevant facts about your customer, planned your territory and done your preliminary work efficiently, you will probably have won an interview with your client.

Before you rush off to meet him however, there's a bit more planning to do.

After all, this is a crucial part of the sales process and first impressions will be important.

I HOPE THIS ISN'T GOING TO BE A WASTE OF TIME...

GOOD AFTERNOON, MR. SMITH!

So, prior to your turning up at the interview, make sure you are clear on these two points:

① CALL OBJECTIVE

② ACTION PLANNING

First, know exactly what you want to come away from the interview with (ie. the Call Objective) and secondly work out how you are going to achieve your objective (your Action Plan).

Much depends on the Buy Phase.

(Remember Buy Phases from Chapter 1 : New Buy, Re-Buy, Modified Re-Buy?)

So, the objective of the interview must bear some relationship to the stage you have arrived at with your customer. It would be unrealistic to hope to close the sale of a complicated and expensive contract at the first meeting.

I'LL RECOMMEND IT TO THE COMMITTEE AT OUR NEXT SESSION ON MONDAY.

RIGHT, I'LL HELP YOU WITH THE PROPOSAL.

PROPOSAL

And it also depends on the level of your contact.

THIS WILL AFFECT EVERY DEPARTMENT ... I'LL GET THE M·D· IN ON THIS!

Important decisions will be deferred upwards.

...OH, AND WHILE YOU'RE HERE, CAN I ORDER SOME MORE VIDEO CASSETTES?

Only with the most routine of repeat orders is it usual to close a sale on the first visit.

So...

YOUR CALL OBJECTIVE SHOULD BE REALISTIC...

Like...

QUOTATION

To present a Quotation.

Or...

I'LL HAVE TO CONSULT MY M·D ON THIS..

To find out who the key executives are and how best you can influence them.

Or...

To get an introduction to the Managing Director.

WHAT ALL OBJECTIVES HAVE IN COMMON IS THAT THEY SHOULD BE SPECIFIC AND THEY SHOULD BE MEASURABLE ... and your Call Objective should be the same.

PLEASED TO MEET YOU, MR. WHEELER.

You should be able to identify whether you have achieved it..

AND **DON'T** COME BACK!

WAP!

...or not, as the case may be.

STEPS
BEHAVIOUR
VISUAL AIDS
VENUE
OPENING

HAVING DECIDED YOUR OBJECTIVE, WORK ON WAYS OF ATTAINING IT —

DEVELOP YOUR ACTION PLAN

Action Planning falls into five parts. Let's take them in turn.

First, work out a series of logical STEPS which you can go through during the forthcoming interview so that you can cover the points you wish to make.

A: Get customer's ATTENTION

B: Stress product or service BENEFITS

C: CLOSE interview.

Try to make up a mnemonic or formula, which will help you remember these steps when you are talking to your customer....

... So that during the interview you will be able to remember the points without having to consult your notes.

GOOD AFTERNOON, MR. CUSTOMER!

WHAT DO YOU WANT?

REMEMBERING MY ABC GIVES ME CONFIDENCE.

STEPS ✓
BEHAVIOUR
VISUAL AIDS
VENUE
OPENING

After you've worked out the steps in the interview, you should determine how you are going to BEHAVE while the interview takes place.

Few people are likely to make the Foolish Salesman's mistakes...

I'M YER MAN, SQUIRE!

... and where it is a good idea to have a firm handshake and a warm smile, it doesn't pay to overdo either.

WHY HULLO THERE!

Exude confidence in your company...

SO GLAD YOU'VE CHOSEN US, MR. BUYER.

Be enthusiastic about it, but try to do it without talking too much.

WELL WE SORT OF MONITOR YOUR COMPANY'S SORT OF PERFORMANCE AND SORT OF MAKE A SORT OF REPORT BEFORE WE SORT OF SUBMIT A SORT OF REPORT...
... SORT OF...

Try to discover your mannerisms and play them down.

Above all, listen to what your client is saying ...

....AND IF IT HADN'T BEEN FOR ME THIS COMPANY WOULD HAVE DISAPPEARED DOWN THE TUBES, OH A GOOD MANY YEARS AGO, BELIEVE ME, AND I'LL GIVE YOU YET ANOTHER GRAPHIC EXAMPLE WHI... ...EMP... OF S... SOME O... ATTITUDES,... ...OU THA... WITH... OUT MY IN...

HMM...VERY INTERESTING

... even if it's off the point.

Summarise the conversation from time to time...

NOW LET ME SEE IF I'VE GOT THIS STRAIGHT... FIRST...

This will demonstrate that you have been listening, will convey your empathy with your client and let you check the accuracy of what he's said.

YOUR BODY LANGUAGE IS OF VITAL IMPORTANCE.
So at all times you should give the impression that what your client is saying is of the utmost importance – even if it's not.

I'M INTERESTED

I'M BORED

One last point about behaviour during the forthcoming interview...

Try to get rid of the desk between you and your client. It makes for easier communication.

The desk is a psychological barrier behind which the client can hide – and it could play a big part in hindering a good working relationship.

STEPS ✓
BEHAVIOUR ✓
VISUAL AIDS
VENUE
OPENING

We now come to the third part of your action-plan: support material & visual aids.

These must be well-presented and RELEVANT

... and be there to reinforce the message you want to deliver **yourself** – never as a substitute.

HELLO MR. BUYER!

Your material should be **controllable**, in good condition, up to date and in a pre-planned order, so that you don't have to apologise for it.

I HAVE A FEW FIGURES HERE...

HELP!

Demonstrations can often be a good idea...

ET VOILÀ.... INSTANT COFFEE... BLUB!

SQUORT!

AT A TOUCH!

...Providing you can be sure they will work properly.

Also, make sure your demonstration successfully illustrates the benefits you are selling...

HANG ON.. I HAD IT A MINUTE AGO...

YOU GET £2,000 £8,000 £1,500 20,000

LIFE INSURANCE POLICY

...and be sure you are the right person to give it — you can always arrange for your technical expert to come with you.

Make sure your audience is the **right one**.

...AND NOW, THE FLOW-RATE OF THE HIGH FREQUENCY VALVE WILL YIELD...

CLIC-GDOING!

So, check on your equipment beforehand. Even if equipment breakdown is not your fault, it impairs your credibility if the demonstration is not smooth.

44

During demonstrations, always explain to the client what's going to happen.

SO, WHEN YOU **SWITCH** ALL YOUR CLERICAL STAFF...

OK, OK...

This way he will be able to understand the significance of your actions.

This understanding is also helped if you break up the demonstration into sections.

YES, THAT'S GOOD, BUT...

This will allow time for anyone to ask questions as the demonstration proceeds, which again aids understanding.

Summarise the demonstration at the end...

NOW, TO SUM UP...

...and try to arrange to leave the clients in the room alone for a while so that they can discuss what they've seen.

Finally...

... Don't forget to thank everyone at the end of the demonstration.

STEPS ✓
BEHAVIOUR ✓
VISUAL AIDS ✓
VENUE
OPENING

I SAID...
HOW DO YOU DO?

EH?

BREEP BREEP

BUZZZ

Bring! Ring

Tweet

DEET DEET

BLEEP

...but this isn't always the **best** place.

Meetings with clients take place, most of the time, in their offices...

AH, THIS IS THE LIFE!

Whether it's in his office or somewhere else, the client ought to be undisturbed when you talk to him, so if you think your talk is going to be interrupted by phone calls or visits from his colleagues...

BROOM CLOSET

I THINK WE'RE OK IN HERE...

...suggest a change of room where you won't be overheard...

...or even invite him out to lunch

NICE QUIET PLACE, THIS!

Now you have his undivided attention...

STEPS ✓
BEHAVIOUR ✓
VISUAL AIDS ✓
VENUE ✓
OPENING

Now we come to the interview itself.

3 Course MENU:
APPEARANCE
PLEASANTRIES
BUSINESS

SHALL WE ORDER?

Menu

First make sure your appearance is **appropriate**, conforming to what is generally expected by people in your business.
Err on the side of restraint; you will be taken more seriously.

3 Course MENU: APPEARANCE PLEASANTRIES BUSINESS

The next item on the menu is the question of pleasantries.

Very few people want to talk business the moment they meet. A short time is usually spent gauging the kind of person they are talking to, and breaking the ice.

Time taken in exchanging pleasantries is rarely time wasted, provided that the time is short.

I WONDER WHAT HE'S LIKE?

I WONDER WHAT HE'S LIKE?

SO...

HOW'S THE WIFE?

WHAT'S IT TO YOU?

... but be careful to avoid giving offence.

Also try not to talk about yourself, but about your customer.

YAWN...

HERE'S ANOTHER GOOD ONE OF AUNTIE...

He's not interested in where you went for your holidays ...

... but it might be a good thing if you were interested in where he went for his.

FASCINATING PLACE, THE WELSH COALFIELDS!

I'M SURE THEY ARE.

But as soon as you can, GET DOWN TO BUSINESS.

IS THAT RIGHT— I HEAR YOU'RE MOVING TO LARGER PREMISES?

... or give some information, refer to a previous visit or produce a sample.

YES, CENTRALISING OUR ACTIVITIES

THEN YOU MAY BE INTERESTED IN OUR NEW...

REALLY, WILL IT HELP US SET UP?

SPECIALLY DESIGNED AND TAILOR-MADE FOR YOU...

Then you will be able to continue the interview along the lines you had planned before the interview.

But don't go on too long...

SO IF I PUT SOME FIGURES IN THE MAIL...

GOOD IDEA!

... and don't forget your objective for this particular meeting, so **CLOSE** as quickly as you can.

One last reminder...

DEAR OLD PALS...

Hic

Hic!

Let your behaviour, like your appearance, err on the side of restraint.

To recap...

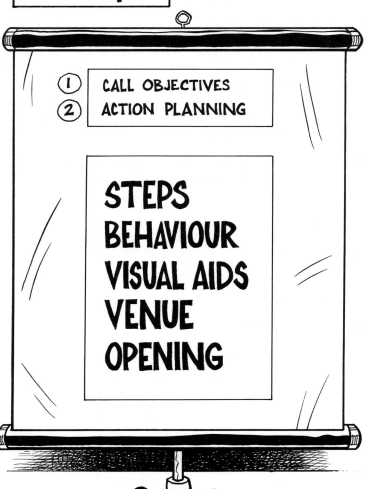

① CALL OBJECTIVES
② ACTION PLANNING

STEPS
BEHAVIOUR
VISUAL AIDS
VENUE
OPENING

Two things need to be understood before the interview : WHAT you want to get out of it, and HOW you intend going about it.

The Action Plan is divided into five parts :

1. The series of logical STEPS which will take you through the interview and which will make sure you cover all the points you want to make.

2. Your BEHAVIOUR during the interview. You should show confidence and restraint. Try to get rid of the desk between you and your client.

3. The SUPPORT MATERIAL you need. Make sure it works and is up to date. Keep it in good order and, during the interview, get rid of it when it's served its purpose.

4. Make sure the VENUE is undisturbed and conducive to business.

5. Decide how you are going to OPEN the discussion of business after the brief pleasantries.

SUGGESTED OPENING STATEMENTS

Here are some suggestions about the way you might have opened the various sales interviews. Remember, these openings are provided as guidelines and your responses do not have to be exactly the same.

Situation 1:   *You are visiting a client company on the heels of an advertising campaign in the national press.*

'Did you see our advertisement in the ... Mr Buyer?'

If the response is *yes:*   'Can you tell me how you reacted to it?'
If the response is *no*   'Well, let me tell you what we are aiming to do.'

The advertisement is a good lever to open the interview. Even a 'No' response can keep the salesman in control of the situation.

Situation 2:   *It is your first meeting with the client*

'Mr Buyer, as we haven't met before, how would it be if I spent a couple of minutes telling you about our company, the services we offer and the impressive results we achieve for our clients? We could then move on to discuss the ways in which we might be able to bring you similar benefits.'

At a first meeting the buyer is likely to feel insecure because there are so many unknowns. This opening removes the insecurity in three ways:

- It provides the offer of necessary background information.
- It offers a structure to the meeting.
- It does not sound as if the salesman is going to waste time.

Situation 3:   *You have submitted a proposal to the client company.*

'Well, Mr Buyer, have you had time to study my proposal?'

If the response is *yes:*   'Perhaps you can tell me what you think of it?'
If the response is *no:*   'Never mind, let me quickly go through it then.'

Clients do not always read proposals as quickly as we would like them to. To make this assumption when the client has not read it could be perceived as an attack on him.

The initial question asked pleasantly and non-critically gives rise to two alternatives, either of which can move the sales interview forward and under control.

Situation 4: *Your organization has developed a new service*

'As you know, Mr Buyer, we have established our reputation by providing a single first-class service. We are now adding another equally fine service to our existing one. Let me tell you about it.'

Talking about the new service in this way reinforces the value of the other earlier service and does not imply that it is now superseded.

Situation 5: *Your contact at the company has been loath to commit himself to a decision despite several earlier meetings*

'Mr Buyer, I'm pleased that you have taken the time to weigh up all the pros and cons of my proposition. Now, perhaps if we can just summarize where we have got to in our discussion, we can then decide how we can progress matters to a favourable solution.'

This is not criticism of the buyer but recognizes the need to recap the situation and perhaps identify any hitherto unvoiced objection.

It also attempts to involve the buyer in the summarizing process and might make it easier to progress to a close.

Situation 6: *There has been a complaint to head office*

'I'm very sorry to hear that you had to complain, Mr Buyer. I'm here to straighten things out if I possibly can. Now as I understand it, what happened was ...'

The response is genuine in its sorrow. The salesman is being as positive as he can in the circumstances. The buyer is now asked to explain all over again why he is complaining, and the salesman demonstrates that people at head office actually listen to complaints and relay them back to the field.

Situation 7: *You are asked to visit a client company at the request of their buyer*

'I'm extremely pleased that you have contacted us, Mr Buyer. Can I ask you how you heard of our service? And what is it exactly you would like to discuss?'

If the request is out of the blue it can be helpful to know how it originated — it can sometimes strengthen the salesman's position by having such information. However, it is wise to move on quickly to finding the reason behind the request by asking a simple question.

Situation 8: *The buyer is an extremely busy person*

'I know you are extremely busy, Mr Buyer, so let's get to the heart of the matter.'

Sometimes 'busyness' is used by buyers as a screen behind which to hide. However, when the time constraints are genuine, there will be no better way of empathizing with the busy buyer than to manage the interview time well.

Situation 9:   *You were given a referral to the client by another customer*

'Well, Mr Buyer, as he might have told you already, your ex-colleague Mr Hones was so impressed by our service that he suggested that I ought to contact you. He felt we might achieve similar savings in your company.'

Having established the reference source, it is advisable to move on to benefits and business matters as quickly as possible, thus avoiding the possible trap of hearing all about their earlier friendship and social lives.

Situation 10:   *You want to establish a long-term contract with an established client*

'I've been checking back and found that over the last five years we have done quite a lot of business together, but in a very spasmodic pattern. Now, what I'm beginning to think, Mr Buyer, is that if we can work out some way of planning ahead when you are likely to need our services, I could possibly save you a lot of money. This is what I have in mind ...'

There are factual and logical reasons for changing the spasmodic individual contracts into perhaps a longer term contract. The benefits to the customer are clearly going to be in terms of money saving and perhaps a reduction in peak demands for the bought-in service.

Exercise 3

THE OPENING STATEMENT

On the following worksheet are listed a number of sales situations which could easily be encountered in day-to-day work. Your task is to imagine that you are actually faced with these situations and to respond to them accordingly.

As we have seen in Chapter 3 each sales interview will invariably commence with some exchange of pleasantries. However, *for the purpose of this exercise*, assume that the pleasantries phase is over and your opening statement will be the first move in the business transaction.

When you have responded to *all* the situations outlined in the worksheet, check your answers against our suggestions, which follow. It is important to remember that it is impossible to be absolutely prescriptive about sales situations such as those described in this exercise. Thus the 'answers' are there in the nature of guidelines, with brief notes to commend them. It will be most unlikely that you come up with exactly the same formulation of words, but if your overall approach is along similar lines, then you should be getting the interview started in a reasonable manner with every prospect of subsequent success.

WORKSHEET

	Imagine that the pleasantries are over and you are about to open these individual and unrelated sales interviews. What would you say? Write your answers on a separate sheet of paper.
Situation 1:	You are visiting a client on the heels of an advertising campaign in the national press.
Situation 2:	It is your first meeting with the client.
Situation 3:	You have submitted a proposal to the client company.
Situation 4:	Your organization has developed a new service.
Situation 5:	Your contact at the company has been loath to commit himself to a decision despite several earlier meetings.
Situation 6:	There has been a complaint to head office.
Situation 7:	You are asked to visit a client company at the request of the buyer.
Situation 8:	The buyer is an extremely busy person.
Situation 9:	You were given a referral to the client by another customer.
Situation 10:	You want to establish a long-term contract with an established client.

Benefit Selling

OUR PRODUCT / SERVICE IS COST-EFFECTIVE

WHICH MEANS THAT

MY COMPANY SAVES **LOTS** OF **MONEY**!

When a salesman reaches agreement with a buyer, you might think that he has sold his services or product.

What he has actually sold is a package of **benefits**.

In this exchange, note the key phrase...

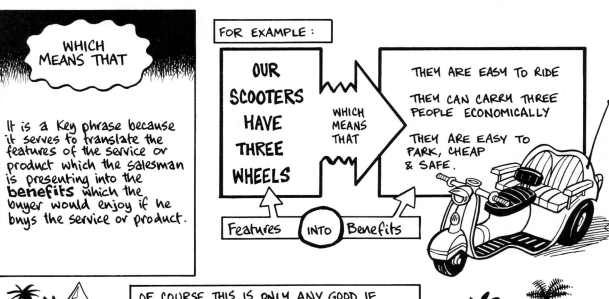

WHICH MEANS THAT

It is a key phrase because it serves to translate the features of the service or product which the salesman is presenting into the **benefits** which the buyer would enjoy if he buys the service or product.

FOR EXAMPLE:

OUR SCOOTERS HAVE THREE WHEELS

WHICH MEANS THAT

THEY ARE EASY TO RIDE

THEY CAN CARRY THREE PEOPLE ECONOMICALLY

THEY ARE EASY TO PARK, CHEAP & SAFE.

Features INTO Benefits

OF COURSE THIS IS ONLY ANY GOOD IF THE BENEFIT **IS** A BENEFIT...

MA, PA —LOOK!

...So the benefits of this product are lost under these circumstances.

GIVE UP, SON.

THE OLD WAYS ARE BEST, MA!

GLUB

Sometimes though, buyers themselves help translate features into benefits...

Take this case:

OUR BREAKDOWN SERVICE OPERATES ANYWHERE IN THE COUNTRY.

The buyer is inviting the salesman to spell out the benefits contained in the feature.

SO WHAT?

In fact he's **challenging** him to **prove** it's a benefit he can't get elsewhere.

IT MEANS YOU CAN GET YOUR CAR FIXED **IN YOUR OWN GARAGE!**

Once again, the benefit had better be a real one to the buyer or the salesman will get a second 'SO WHAT?' which may be less easy to respond to.

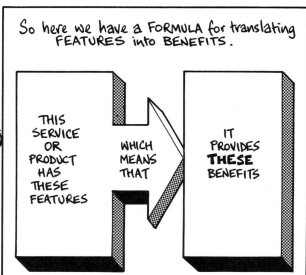

So here we have a FORMULA for translating FEATURES into BENEFITS.

THIS SERVICE OR PRODUCT HAS THESE FEATURES

WHICH MEANS THAT

IT PROVIDES **THESE** BENEFITS

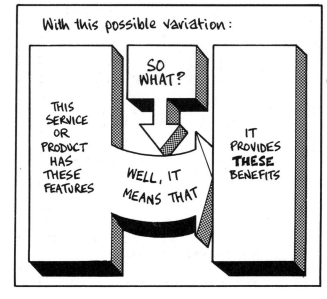

With this possible variation:

THIS SERVICE OR PRODUCT HAS THESE FEATURES

SO WHAT?

WELL, IT MEANS THAT

IT PROVIDES **THESE** BENEFITS

REMEMBER...

...AND THE FREEZER IS COMPLETELY STOCKED WITH TV DINNERS

The salesman has to be sure what benefits he can offer, and whether they are really going to **BE** benefits to his customer.

He should analyse his service or his product, and identify all its features and its benefits, first of all collecting all the relevant facts for each of his customers:

BENEFIT ANALYSIS SHEET				
CUSTOMER APPEAL (This column is to help show what issues/features are of particular concern to the customer).	FEATURES (Describes what the product or service is).	ADVANTAGES (Describes what it does).	BENEFITS (Describes what the customer gets **that he needs**).	PROOF (Gives evidence that the benefit can be realised).
e.g	e.g	e.g	e.g	e.g
'Is looking for cost-effective coating for range of kitchenware manufacture'.	TEFLON	NON-STICK EASY SPRAY APPLICATION	TROUBLE-FREE COOKING EASIER WASHING UP etc...	NAMES OF OTHER COMPANIES RELATED APPLICATIONS eg. SPACE AGENCIES
OR				
'Wants to widen credit facilities'.	ACCESS CREDIT CARD	PROVIDES CREDIT FACILITIES WORLDWIDE	ELIMINATES NEED TO CARRY CASH EASES CASHFLOW PROBLEMS etc...	PERHAPS INDEPENDENT FINANCIAL ANALYSES

A Benefit Analysis sheet will help you conduct the necessary analysis and relate it to the individual customer's needs.

But let's now look a bit more closely at what a **benefit** is.
Not all benefits are the same...

We can divide them into three categories:

Standard Benefits
Company Benefits
Differential Benefits

The examples we've already looked at are **standard benefits**.

I SAID...

IT MEANS YOU CAN GET YOUR CAR FIXED **IN YOUR OWN GARAGE!**

I **LOVE** IT!

Standard Benefits arise from the nature of the product or service itself, and in selling standard benefits the salesman must remember to mention **all** the benefits, not just the ones which he thinks are special.

For instance...

...OH, YOU GET THE NORMAL BREAKDOWN SERVICE TOO — **PLUS** FREE CAR HIRE **AND** YOUR OWN CAR TOWED TO THE NEAREST REPAIR CENTRE IF NECESSARY.

REALLY?

Here the salesman is spelling out the benefits the customer could normally expect from such a service.

It's important to do this, otherwise the buyer might harbour doubts about it...

DO I HAVE TO PAY THE BREAKDOWN MAN?

WHAT ABOUT **FLEET** RATES?

...and any unanswered questions might get in the way of a sale.

So, remember to mention **every** benefit of your service.

Which brings us to the second kind of benefit...

Company Benefits

Unlike standard benefits, which are associated with the product or service on offer, Company Benefits concern the relationship between the selling company and the buying company.

Company Benefits arise from the degree of dependence of the buyer on the seller, and the more confidence the buyer has in the seller, the more important company benefits become.

In selling a Company Benefit, the seller might say something like this:

HERE, MR. BUYER, WE CAN HANDLE ALL YOUR CORPORATE TRAVEL ARRANGEMENTS.

TRAVEL PACKAGE

WHAT MAKES YOU SO **SURE?**

BECAUSE, LIKE YOU, WE HAVE AN OFFICE IN THE UNITED STATES

WHICH MEANS THAT

WE CAN SERVICE YOUR OVERSEAS OPERATION ON THE **SAME TERMS**

WHICH MEANS THAT

YOU WILL BE ABLE TO CONTROL YOUR TRAVEL EXPENDITURE FROM YOUR HQ HERE.

So, what's being sold is not just the product or service, but the selling organisation too. This means that the salesman must include any after-sales service he can offer in his range of benefits.

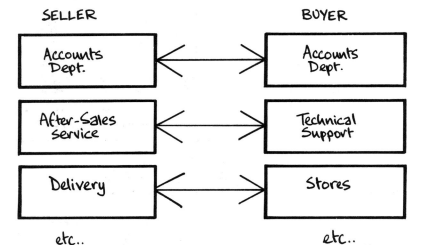

When a buying company recognises and accepts the Company Benefits of the supplier, links can be forged between relevant departments of the two companies.

Obviously this is a desirable situation from the supplying company's point of view, and the buyer will have to have a lot of confidence in the supplier if this is to happen.

The buyer will be concerned about the selling company's reputation, how good its staff are, how it can cope with changing circumstances, and whether it's going to provide the service it promises.

Remember, even when you are selling products, there's a service element involved, and selling a service is a matter of faith.

It's up to the salesman to inspire the faith.

We now come to the third kind of benefits:

Matches

READY-LIT MATCHES

DIFFERENTIAL BENEFITS

Remember this example?

OUR BREAKDOWN SERVICE OPERATES **ANYWHERE** IN THE **COUNTRY**

WHICH MEANS THAT

YOU CAN GET YOUR CAR FIXED **IN YOUR OWN GARAGE!**

Said like this, it is a Standard Benefit.

But like this...

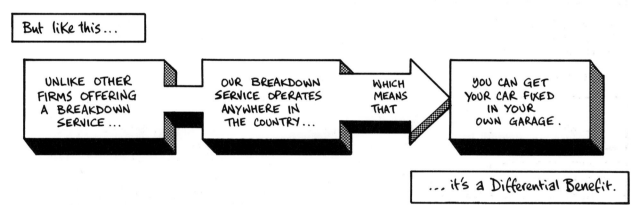

UNLIKE OTHER FIRMS OFFERING A BREAKDOWN SERVICE...

OUR BREAKDOWN SERVICE OPERATES ANYWHERE IN THE COUNTRY...

WHICH MEANS THAT

YOU CAN GET YOUR CAR FIXED IN YOUR OWN GARAGE.

... it's a Differential Benefit.

In other words, the Differential Benefit is measured against the performance of the opposition — and in a market where there may be a number of companies offering a similar kind of service, the Differential Benefit can be the most effective way of closing a sale.

Using Differential Benefits may turn an apparent **disadvantage** into an **advantage**

as follows...

Video production companies are usually based in big cities, but as the production services on which they depend become more widespread and as urban overheads rise, more production companies work from outside, travelling in when required to meet their city customers...

... so turning a Standard Benefit ...

... into a Differential Benefit.

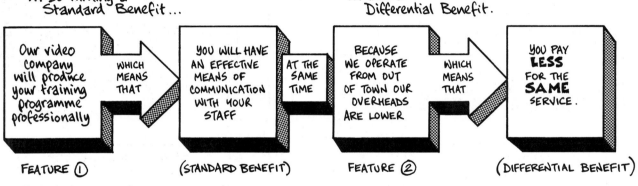

| Our video company will produce your training programme professionally | WHICH MEANS THAT | YOU WILL HAVE AN EFFECTIVE MEANS OF COMMUNICATION WITH YOUR STAFF | AT THE SAME TIME | BECAUSE WE OPERATE FROM OUT OF TOWN OUR OVERHEADS ARE LOWER | WHICH MEANS THAT | YOU PAY **LESS** FOR THE **SAME** SERVICE. |

FEATURE ①   (STANDARD BENEFIT)   FEATURE ②   (DIFFERENTIAL BENEFIT)

DIFFERENTIAL BENEFITS ARE THOSE WHICH PROVIDE A **COMPETITIVE EDGE** OVER RIVAL COMPANIES' BENEFITS.

They spell out the unique quality of the product or service and are therefore the **Key** to the company's success. So it's important for the salesman to identify what his company's differential benefits are.

Of the services offered by these three salesmen, the one on the right is obviously the best - if he can prove it.

But... ... what if there were only these two?

CHEAPER

BETTER

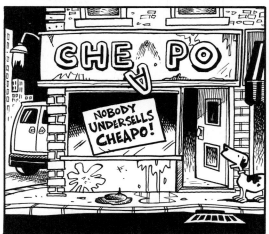

CHEAPO

NOBODY UNDERSELLS CHEAPO!

Different kinds of benefits will appeal to different customers, so one of these will satisfy one need and perhaps the other will satisfy another.

Important: Establish your customers **needs**

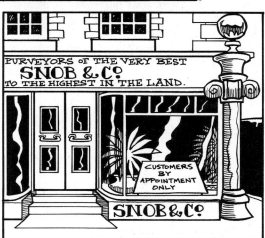

PURVEYORS OF THE VERY BEST
SNOB & C⁰
TO THE HIGHEST IN THE LAND.

CUSTOMERS BY APPOINTMENT ONLY

SNOB & C⁰

COMMUNICATING BENEFITS:

When explaining benefits to your clients, make sure you are understood. Unless you can talk the 'buyer's language', all your preparatory work will be in vain— So:

① Keep it simple; don't be like the man on the left.

THERE'S A MALFUNCTION IN YOUR HUMAN RESOURCES, RESULTING IN A LOCALISED CAPACITY DEFICIENCY IN YOUR MANUFACTURING FACILITY.

HE MEANS "THERE'S TROUBLE AT MILL", BOSS

② Avoid jargon; unless the buyer is able to speak it.

...SQUARE-WAVE MODULATION AT PLUS OR MINUS 4 RAUS WITHOUT SURGE...

YES, BUT WILL IT DO THE JOB?

③ Avoid value words.

...SO THESE CHEAP FAKES WILL CON THE SUCKERS INTO BELIEVING THEY'RE BUYING PROPER WATCHES...

OH DEAR!

The salesman needs to be aware of words which could be interpreted as an attack on the buyer's values.

④ Be positive.

OUR EXPERIENCE SHOWS THAT THE SUCCESS RATE OF A SCHEME LIKE THIS IS OVER 50%, AND THAT'S **GOOD**.

I'M AFRAID THAT THIS KIND OF SCHEME FAILS HALF THE TIME.

One of these statements is more positive than the other. No prizes for guessing which.

⑤ Be active.(ie. not passive)

THIS

I CAN SHOW YOU THE BENEFITS OF THIS PRODUCT

NOT THIS

THE BENEFITS OF THIS PRODUCT CAN BE DEMONSTRATED

⑥ Try to select your environment.

NICE TO SEE YOU AGAIN!

Quiet surroundings, no desk barrier, a relaxed atmosphere — all contribute to success.

TO SUM UP...

* Customers do not buy a service or a product — they buy the benefits these bring:

* Salesmen must therefore:

— identify the benefits of their product or service.

— ask questions to find out what benefits the customer needs.

— make a sales offer in terms of these benefits.

— ask further questions to gain responses about customer appeal.

— communicate clearly, concisely & effectively... & ... **ALWAYS TALK BENEFITS**.

MORE ABOUT COMMUNICATING WITH YOUR CLIENT IN THE NEXT CHAPTER.

Exercise 4

BENEFIT ANALYSIS OF YOUR OWN PRODUCTS OR SERVICES

This exercise has been designed to help you to apply Chapter 4 to your own special circumstances, using your own products or services as the learning vehicle.

Step 1   Remind yourself about what is involved in completing a benefit analysis sheet by studying the following form. If necessary, look back at Chapter 4 for an illustration of what benefits are.

Step 2   Using the blank benefit analysis sheet that follows complete it for a potentially major customer for your product or service.

Step 3   Make brief notes about how you will approach this potentially major customer, your opening statements, and how you will introduce the major benefits to them.

BENEFIT ANALYSIS SHEET

Customer				
Products or services required				
Customer appeal	Features	Advantages	Benefits	Proof

Objections

A: Get customer's ATTENTION

B: Stress product or service BENEFITS

C: CLOSE interview.

In chapter 3 the salesman used a memory jogger to remember the stages of a sales interview.

But it doesn't always work as simply as ABC...

YES, BUT...

Somewhere along the line, the buyer will start raising objections.

Unless he has already decided to buy your product or your service, in spite of what you might do or say, objections are almost inevitable at one point or another — and they are not necessarily a bad thing.

At some stage of the sale, particularly if the product or service being offered is complex, the buyer is bound to be uncertain about some points.

...WILL SOLVE YOUR DATA CONTROL PROBLEMS..

YES, BUT CAN I WRITE **LETTERS** ON IT?

If these doubts and uncertainties remain unresolved, they could undermine the buyer's confidence.

The customer's uncertainty could endanger the sale, so...

...AND IT'S TERRIFIC FOR WRITING LETTERS.

The salesman must be able to **sense** an objection before it comes, but **once spoken**...

YES, BUT IT'S NOT COMPATIBLE WITH OUR CURRENT WORD PROCESSORS

... the objection becomes a **barrier** to a successful sale.

So first of all try to anticipate what the objections to your proposal are likely to be...

I CAN GIVE YOU TEN MINUTES — I'VE GOT A MOUNTAIN OF WORK TO GET THROUGH!

...and frame a proposal so that the likely objections are countered...

OUR COMPUTER-BASED INFORMATION CONTROL SYSTEM CLEARS THE PAPERWORK FROM YOUR DESK — JUST LIKE THE PERFECT SECRETARY!

WHY DON'T YOU LET US INSTALL IT AND TRAIN YOUR STAFF FOR A WEEK. IF YOU DON'T LIKE IT WE'LL TAKE IT AWAY.

YOU RANG, SIR?

BUT IF AN OBJECTION IS RAISED, YOU **MUST** ANSWER IT.

IT'S GREAT! BUT I CAN'T AFFORD IT.

WRITING IT OFF AGAINST YOUR BUSINESS OVER TEN YEARS, IT COMES OUT AT ABOUT £4 PER 24 HOUR DAY (IT DOESN'T SLEEP OR NEED FOOD) WHICH IS ABOUT 16p PER HOUR — AND IT'S TAX DEDUCTABLE OF COURSE.

An objection may not signify sales resistance, merely the buyer's way of **asking questions** — and they could help the salesman identify the buyer's genuine concern. So....

ANALYSE THE OBJECTION.

It can probably be turned to your advantage. Objections fall into two categories:

FUNDAMENTAL OBJECTIONS

STANDARD OBJECTIONS

A FUNDAMENTAL OBJECTION is raised when the buyer does not see the need for the product or service being offered.

This is no time for benefit selling. The buyer has to be convinced that he **actually does have a need**.

YOU MEAN YOU CAN DO WITHOUT **PLANNING?**

The FUTURE

NOT INTERESTED

Here of course, the salesman really **is** selling benefits — but in a different form, by describing what the situation will be without the help of the seller's service or product.

As ever, the salesman must do his homework.

YOUR RETAINED PROFIT WOULD HAVE BEEN UP 50% USING US, LET ME SHOW YOU...

CLIENT'S ANNUAL REPORT

You must know that what you are offering will benefit the buyer.

IT IS NO GOOD TRYING TO COUNTER A FUNDAMENTAL OBJECTION IF THE OBJECTION IS A VALID ONE.

SO **THERE!** HA! HA! YOU'RE **WRONG!**

But in countering objections the salesman runs the risk of proving the buyer wrong, which may cause even greater barriers.

The salesman must exercise tact when countering objections.

I SEE YOUR COMPANY DID VERY WELL LAST YEAR. STILL...

CLIENT'S ANNUAL REPORT

If he can appear to agree with the customer, so much the better.

Now for the second kind of objection. The... STANDARD OBJECTION.

SAL

IT'S OK... **BUT...**

I DON'T LIKE IT.

Standard objections are of many kinds, the most common of which are these six....

FEATURE OBJECTIONS

LACK·OF·KNOWLEDGE OBJECTIONS

DELAY OBJECTIONS

HIDDEN OBJECTIONS

LOYALTY OBJECTIONS

PRICE OBJECTIONS

The first of these, FEATURE OBJECTIONS, can largely be avoided if, once again, the salesman has done his homework.

The product or the service will have been offered in the first place because it genuinely contains benefits for the buyer, so the salesman should be aware of the buyer's needs at this stage, and in the case of a service, it might well have been designed with that buyer in mind.

BRILLIANT SCHEME

THIS SCHEME WILL WORK IN **ALL** YOUR BRANCHES, IN YOUR WAREHOUSES **AND** IN YOUR **HEAD OFFICE!**

AHA... YES... I **GET IT**!

I THINK...

Of course the buyer may not have grasped all the implications of the seller's proposal...

...which brings us to the LACK-OF-KNOWLEDGE OBJECTION.

NO... IT WON'T WORK.

Though this sometimes **sounds** like a FEATURE OBJECTION, it's different because it's rooted in the buyer's lack of understanding.

Objections like this are to be welcomed by the salesman because the buyer is still interested — though he somehow feels there's a drawback.

EXTRA BENEFITS

BIGGER RETURN ON INVESTMENT

SAVINGS IN TIME

All the salesman now has to do is demonstrate that the objection has no substance. In fact he might be able to **close the sale** at this point, like this...

IF I CAN ARRANGE IT SO THAT YOU PAY THE **SAME** PREMIUM, WOULD YOU GO AHEAD WITH THE SCHEME?

If the buyer says 'yes' to this question, the sale has been closed.

The third kind of STANDARD OBJECTION contains the element of DELAY...

I'LL HAVE TO ASK THE COMMITTEE

This is a difficult one to cope with because it seems a reasonable thing for the buyer to do. After all, it could be genuine.

I'LL STALL HIM WHILE I MAKE UP MY MIND...

On the other hand, it could be a means of avoiding making a decision for some other reason. It could be the buyer is still not convinced, or that he genuinely needs time to think. Or, there could be yet another reason....

67

THE HIDDEN OBJECTION.

YOU SAID THAT PRICE IS NOT A PROBLEM, SO — YOUR OTHER REASON FOR NOT DECIDING IS....?

The salesman can sometimes find out what this is by using an incomplete question and waiting for the buyer to complete the sentence.

ER, WELL... I'M REALLY WORRIED ABOUT BEING LEFT WITHOUT AFTER-SALES SERVICE IF YOUR FIRM GOES BUST...

This frequently has the effect of unearthing the buyer's **real** objection, which will enable the salesman to counter it and to move on to close the sale. The secret is to ask a question which must be answered by a statement and not a straight 'no'.

The next kind of objection is...

THE LOYALTY OBJECTION.

BEEN USING SCROGGS HERE FOR FIFTEEN YEARS NOW!

The LOYALTY OBJECTION is an expression of the buyer's confidence in his existing supplier.

This is a real challenge to the salesman.

DO NOT KNOCK THE OPPOSITION

NICE LITTLE CHAP!

It would amount to an attack on the buyer's judgement. Here the salesman must be patient.

First of all, offer your service as a safeguard.

I CAN UNDERSTAND YOUR LOYALTY TO A RELIABLE SUPPLIER, AND I APPRECIATE IT. HOWEVER, YOU CAN USE US AS A YARDSTICK TO SEE IF HE IS CONTINUING TO GIVE GOOD VALUE — AND IF YOU ARE IN A FIX YOU CAN FALL BACK ON US.

This will not commit the buyer.

Then, find good reasons for returning to see him...

ONE WEEK LATER:

THOUGHT I'D DROP IN AND SHOW YOU OUR LATEST...

NEW RANGE

Such persistence pays, particularly when the service or product on offer exceeds that given by the existing supplier.

Here's the last kind of STANDARD OBJECTION:

HOW MUCH DID YOU SAY?

For many buyers, the objection concerns the PRICE of the product or service.

OCCASIONALLY IT IS GENUINE, but...

WHAT DO I GET FOR IT?

... more often than not he is not so much interested in price as in VALUE FOR MONEY.

IT'S GOOD, BUT CAN I SWING IT WITH THE FINANCE DEPARTMENT?

He will probably have to justify his decisions with other members of the DECISION MAKING UNIT, and the quality of what's on offer will have to correspond to the price asked.

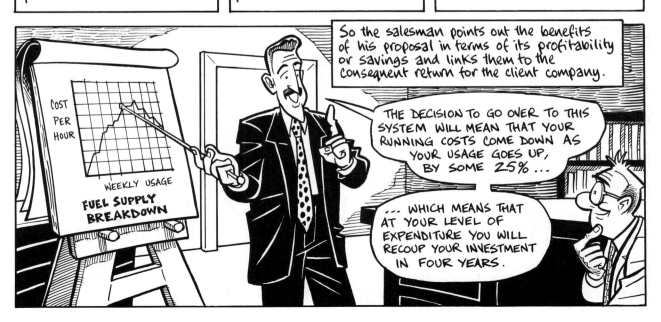

COST PER HOUR

WEEKLY USAGE

FUEL SUPPLY BREAKDOWN

So the salesman points out the benefits of his proposal in terms of its profitability or savings and links them to the consequent return for the client company.

THE DECISION TO GO OVER TO THIS SYSTEM WILL MEAN THAT YOUR RUNNING COSTS COME DOWN AS YOUR USAGE GOES UP, BY SOME 25% ...

... WHICH MEANS THAT AT YOUR LEVEL OF EXPENDITURE YOU WILL RECOUP YOUR INVESTMENT IN FOUR YEARS.

At the same time the salesman can diminish the price objection by stating it in other terms, breaking down the costs into the smallest terms possible.

PUT IT THIS WAY— THE SCHEME COSTS **ONLY** ONE HOUR PER WORKER PER WEEK.

Notice the use of the word 'only'

HMM... S'RIGHT ENOUGH...

TAP TAP

But the buyer can make use of 'only' too!

AHA! SCROGGS IS **ONLY** NINE TENTHS OF THE PRICE!

So... if he compares your price with the opposition's you should be prepared to offer him differential benefits based on **value for money.**

YES, SCROGGS IS 10 PER CENT CHEAPER, **BUT...**

FOR THIS EXTRA 10 PER CENT YOU GET 25 PER CENT SAVINGS ON RUNNING COSTS, 50 PER CENT SAVING ON SPARE PARTS...

WHICH MEANS AN OVERALL SAVING OF 30 PER CENT OVER THE LIFE OF THE PRODUCT.

There is a RIGHT TIME to introduce the price element to the buyer.

SO YOU GET ALL THESE BENEFITS FROM THE SCHEME ... AND THE PRICE...

It comes at the **end** of the explanation of all the benefits because it enables the salesman to **justify** the cost.
However...

... the buyer might ask the price earlier than you want.

G'MORNING SI'DOWN — **HOW MUCH?**

If you know, you must tell him and deal with the situation from there

70

TOO MUCH!

WELL, LET ME TELL YOU WHAT YOU GET...

At least take comfort that the buyer will not raise a Fundamental Objection. His question about price implies that he is interested in your service.

But if you don't know the price, tell the buyer why.

IT'S GOING TO DEPEND...

It's because you need more information. This could be an advantage in disguise because the situation could develop where you could now CLOSE THE SALE.

SO IF WE CAN SATISFY THESE POINTS AND GET THE PRICE RIGHT, COULD WE GO FORWARD...?

'Getting the price right' means selling your product or service package at more than the minimum you had determined before the interview took place — so **don't offer a discount unless all else fails.**

Otherwise...

OK, SO, ER.. I PAY YOU!

DONE!

The important thing about countering price objections is not to sell yourself short, so do talk about **value** and not **price.**

TO SUM UP THIS CHAPTER:

WORRY
DOUBT
ANXIETY

YES.. ..BUT..

Objections are not necessarily bad things. They reveal the real concerns of the buyer and can therefore be used to the advantage of the salesman.

There are two kinds of objections:

FUNDAMENTAL OBJECTIONS.

STANDARD OBJECTIONS.

Fundamental Objections are those which question the need for the product or service and need to be answered by referring to the disadvantages of not using it.

Standard Objections have six main categories:

FEATURE OBJECTIONS
LACK-OF-KNOWLEDGE OBJECTIONS
DELAY OBJECTIONS
HIDDEN OBJECTIONS
LOYALTY OBJECTIONS
PRICE OBJECTIONS

Voicing Objections is often a buyer's way of asking questions, so the various ways of benefit selling are appropriate ways of answering these.

Exercise 5

OBJECTION ANALYSIS

Make a list of the most common objections you experience in your work. We will now proceed to analyse them using the technique described in Chapter 5 and see how they might be forestalled and countered.

For the moment, try to put your usual responses to the back of your mind and react to each objection in the way this analysis technique leads you. This is not to suggest that your usual responses are necessarily wrong, but to go into this exercise with preconceived notions will clearly reduce the chances of developing any new ideas.

Step 1 Refer back to Chapter 5 and recap on the section about objection analysis. Using the worksheet which follows, enter the name or description of the particular product or service under consideration at the top of the page.

Step 2 Transfer the most common objections to the left-hand column of the worksheet.

Step 3 Analyse each objection in turn and identify its nature, e.g. feature, price, fundamental, hidden, etc. Write your decision in the second column on the worksheet.

Step 4 Taking the most common objection at the top of your list (which you have now categorized into an objection type) write down the words you would use to forestall the client raising this objection. Enter your response or responses in the third column of the worksheet. Continue across the page into the next column and write down how you would now respond to this objection if it were raised. Again more than one response is permissible.

Step 5 Repeat Step 4 for all the remaining objections listed on the worksheet. Use separate sheets of notepaper if the printed worksheet is not large enough for your needs.

Step 6 When you have completed the worksheet, look back on what you have written. In those cases where you have listed more than one response in the 'forestalling' or 'answer' columns, underline the response that you think will be the most effective. These clearly will become useful 'tools' in future sales interviews.

Step 7 Finally, check and see if the ways that you would now answer the most common objections differ from the way you had been answering them in the past. Make any notes that will remind you of useful points that emerged from this exercise and will help you in the future.

OBJECTION ANALYSIS WORKSHEET

Type of product or service

Most common objections (typical words that are used)	The type of objection e.g. feature, price	Ways to forestall objection (try writing what you would say)	Ways to answer objection (write what you would say)

Note: Remember the impact of customer appeal in your replies.

Closing the Sale

And now... we come to the moment the salesman has been preparing for...

SIGN THERE!

... the point at which he **closes the sale**.

This is why he **organised his territory**...

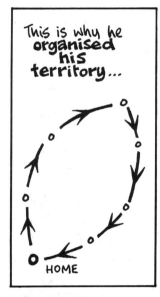

HOME

... prepared for his interview and gained an **appointment**...

WE CAN DO THIS...

... used his **opening techniques**...

WHICH MEANS THAT

... explained his service in terms of **benefits**,...

...and dealt with **objections**.

YES, BUT...

PROPOSAL

He has planned every stage of the selling process with **only one thing in mind**...

I'LL BUY IT!

SMAK!

But, to close a sale successfully, the salesman must have certain techniques at his disposal, which we'll look at in this chapter.

First though, when is a sale **actually closed?**

74

Not at this point ...

GOODBYE! I WILL SEND YOU MY ORDER!

...and certainly not at this point...

DROP IN NEXT WEEK!

But at **this** point, when the customer signs on the dotted line.

ABC PRO
ORDER
Please supply:

Quantity	Code
1	Type 337D
	Rolls code 5549
14	Type 2490 (with A-5)
2	ABC-1 System + 5FW

Signed: Meg Smith

We've seen all the steps leading up to the signing of the order, but this doesn't mean that the salesman will have to go through the whole process every time...

AH! GLAD TO SEE YOU. I NEED SOME MORE OF THE X24 KEYBOARDS. AND CAN YOU GET...

BUYER

Here he can make a sale virtually at the start of the meeting.

In fact...

WAIT A MINUTE WHILE I EXPLAIN THE BENEFITS...

?

The X-24 Information Item

...he would be very foolish if he tried to go through the whole process again, because the customer might harbour doubts about the salesman's seriousness or the competence of his company.

On the other hand it is equally important not to try to close **too** early. A buyer who is not ready to close might well refuse, and this could spoil all the excellent work so far.

HOW ABOUT IT?

So when is the **right** time to close?

PLEASE, OH **PLEASE** SELL ME YOUR SERVICE!

The salesman must look out for signs that the customer is ready to buy. Such buying signs can express themselves in body language...

GO ON, **GO ON!**

... for instance, the customer may suddenly take a very close interest in what you are saying, leaning forward...

... looking closely at your sales literature without being asked — or he may stop doodling at a certain point and become more attentive.

GO OVER THIS BIT AGAIN...

SCHEME

There are other signs...

LOOKS OK...

BUT CAN YOU PROVIDE IT IN TIME?

... for instance, the buyer might raise an objection which conveys his acceptance, as long as he can be reassured on one point. The salesman can then close the sale.

Sometimes, though, the salesman is unable to detect any buying signals. To attempt a close might be dangerous.

So he makes something called: **A TRIAL CLOSE**

For instance, here's a buyer exhibiting a negative attitude:

DUNNO...

... TOO EXPENSIVE, TIME-CONSUMING, COMPLICATED...

The salesman doesn't know whether the objections are genuine or merely **excuses** for prevaricating.

What the salesman does is this...

BUT SUPPOSE I COULD PROVE IT WILL SAVE YOU TIME & MONEY, **WOULD YOU GO AHEAD THEN?**

In other words he makes a proposal which counters the objections, phrased so that a rejection would **not be disastrous**

Another kind of trial close can follow a question from the buyer.

WILL I GET A DISCOUNT IF I PAY PROMPTLY?

The salesman who just answers 'yes' to this question is missing an opportunity to close the deal — or at the very least make a **trial close** which will reveal the buyer's attitude.
He should say something like this...

77

YES, IF YOU PAY IN 30 DAYS WE'LL GIVE YOU 5% DISCOUNT...

Followed by:

IS THAT HOW YOU'D LIKE TO PAY?

The answer to the question will tell the salesman a lot and if the answer is 'Yes', he can move in and close the sale.

Then there's the ALTERNATIVE CLOSE:

HOW WOULD YOU LIKE THIS POLICY?..

...WITH OR WITHOUT BENEFITS?

Whichever choice the buyer makes, the salesman will be able to close. But this course of action is best only if the salesman is reasonably sure he is close to making a sale...

... otherwise it might backfire...

I DON'T WANT EITHER!

... and the sale could be **jeopardised**.

Here's a trial close which uses The **Direct Question**

MR. BUYER, IS THERE ANYTHING ELSE WE CAN DO TO GET YOU TO BUY FROM US?

This risks the answer 'I'm afraid not' (which at least saves time), but it often provokes a response which would give an opportunity to **close**.

Another close is the **summary**.

OK, LET'S SUMMARISE WHAT WE HAVE TO OFFER...

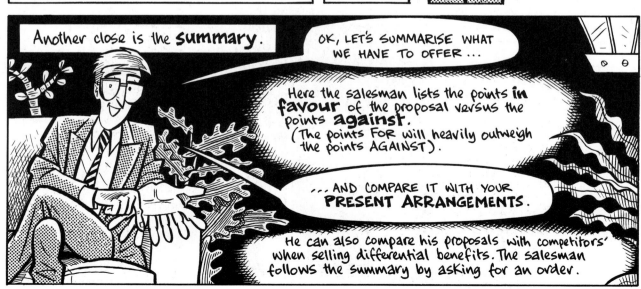

Here the salesman lists the points **in favour** of the proposal versus the points **against**.
(The points FOR will heavily outweigh the points AGAINST).

...AND COMPARE IT WITH YOUR **PRESENT ARRANGEMENTS.**

He can also compare his proposals with competitors' when selling differential benefits. The salesman follows the summary by asking for an order.

One more form of trial close: **using concessions.**

BECAUSE I **LIKE YOU!**

ORDER

£4,000.00
£3,500.00

Discounts, extended guarantees or credit periods, free back-up facilities etc.. can be offered if the sale is **otherwise in doubt.**

But if you offer them at all, do so **late in the discussion...**

MORE, MORE! I WANT **MORE!**

...otherwise their negotiating power might be lost as the meeting progresses.

The last kind of trial close involves **quotations...**

BUYER

If the salesman's **objective** is to get permission to send a quotation and he succeeds, it is a close. Otherwise, a quotation is not an order. It does not commit the buyer to anything...

SEND ME A **QUOTATION** FIRST!

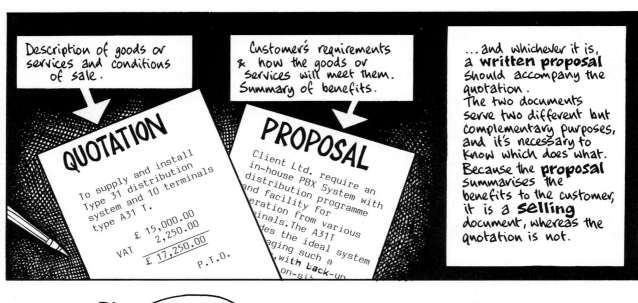

Description of goods or services and conditions of sale.

Customer's requirements & how the goods or services will meet them. Summary of benefits.

...and whichever it is, a **written proposal** should accompany the quotation.
The two documents serve two different but complementary purposes, and it's necessary to know which does what.
Because the **proposal** summarises the benefits to the customer, it is a **selling** document, whereas the quotation is not.

QUOTATION

To supply and install Type 31 distribution system and 10 terminals type A31 T.

£ 15,000.00
2,250.00
VAT ———————
£ 17,250.00
P.T.O.

PROPOSAL

Client Ltd. require an in-house PBX System with distribution programme and facility for ...eration from various ...inals. The A31T ...des the ideal system ...aging such a ...with back-up ...on-si...

GOOD MORNING. NICE TO SEE YOU!

The proposal and the quotation should be followed up by a visit by the salesman to answer queries and, of course, to ask for an order.

Trial closes are like stepping stones to finding out what the buyer **really** wants.

YES, YOU CAN COME AND SEE ME.

The salesman arrives at the first stepping stone when he manages to get an appointment with the buyer.

YES, I AGREE OUR PERFORMANCE COULD IMPROVE.

The second step is when the salesman and buyer **agree** on the problem area.

YES, I APPROVE OF YOUR SERVICE/PRODUCT.

The next stepping stone towards closing a sale is when the kind of service or product on offer is **approved**.

YES, OUR MANAGERS ARE KEEN TO LEARN

OR

YES, OUR MANAGERS WANT TO INCREASE PRODUCTIVITY.

YES, THEY NEED TO KNOW MORE ABOUT MAN-MANAGEMENT

OR

YES, THEY ARE PREPARED TO REVIEW EXISTING PROCEDURES

Then comes the step when the buyer can fit the service or product to his company's specific needs ...

...and perhaps starts outlining some objectives towards greater efficiency...

YES, WE CAN GET THEM ALL TOGETHER AFTER THE SUMMER HOLIDAY PERIOD.

OR

YES, WE CAN BEGIN OUR REVIEW OF PROCEDURES AFTER THE HOLIDAY PERIOD.

CLOSE

...and when the buyer starts working out the practicalities of using the salesman's product or service, the deal is almost closed...

CLOSE

YES, WE'LL **HAVE IT!**

Each stepping stone has represented a small commitment on the way to closing the deal – each commitment being secured by means of a **trial close**.

Exercise 6

OPPORTUNITIES TO CLOSE

As you have read in Chapter 6 the successful salesman does not try to go right through his prepared presentation come what may. Instead, he is constantly on the look out for short cuts that lead to a close (*buying signals*). It is not always easy to recognize a buying signal when it crops up and yet to be successful, we have to learn not only to spot the signal immediately, but also to respond in a natural-sounding way quite spontaneously.

This exercise will enable you to practise the skills of identifying opportunities to close and working out the best way to respond to them.

Read 'The Garden Wall' case study below and answer these questions:

1. Did Derek James, the salesman, miss any buying signals and hence opportunities to close the sale?

2. If he did, at which stage or stages of the interview did opportunities occur?

3. If you had been in Derek James' shoes, how would you have responded to the buying signals you identified in 2 above?

Write your answers down on a separate sheet of notepaper and when you are satisfied with what you have written, turn to our suggested answer, which follows, and check how your answers compare with ours.

The Garden Wall

Derek James was a jobbing builder who undertook a variety of work, from building home extensions to relatively minor house repairs and alterations. Most of his jobs were generated by an advertisement he placed regularly in the local newspaper, the rest by word of mouth.

It was through the former medium that Colin Barrett had got to know of James. Barrett was looking for someone to build a decorative wall in the garden of his home. He had contacted three local builders with a view to comparing their estimates for the job.

James was the first of the three to be seen. Barrett's initial impressions in talking to James over the phone were completely favourable and unknown to James he was already a strong candidate for obtaining the order. It all now depended on how he handled the sales interview. What follows is a transcript of that meeting.

James: Hello, Mr Barrett? I'm Derek James. You wanted to talk to me about some building work.

Barrett: Ah yes. Thank you for coming so promptly. Now what I'm looking for is a small

	decorative retaining wall round that section of raised garden over there. (He points to the area.) Can you give me an estimate for how much it will cost?
James:	Certainly ... and I don't charge for giving an estimate. But I need to know a little bit more about the job first. For example, do you have a special type of brick or colour in mind?
Barrett:	Actually we're not too sure. My wife would prefer to have bricks that match the rest of the house. I would really prefer something a little more rustic.
James:	Well, let me try to help you. If you use normal housebricks like the others, they are only made to "weather" on the face. If they are used as a retaining wall, there is a problem that they soak up water and when the frosts come they start to flake and crack. Ornamental bricks on the other hand don't absorb water — but they are much more expensive.
Barrett:	Oh dear! I didn't really want to spend too much. After all we don't live out in the garden do we?
James:	Yes, I understand Mr Barrett. But the ornamental bricks will last for ages and they will provide a most attractive feature in your garden.
Barrett:	Mmm. Are these bricks easy to get hold of? Now that we've made up our mind to do something, we would like to get things moving quickly.
James:	I'd imagine they would be in stock, unless you wanted something quite unusual. Generally the capping pieces need to be ordered though. That might cause a delay.

Pause

Barrett:	Well, getting back to the bricks idea. Can anything be done to stop them absorbing water?
James:	Yes. I was going to say that if a plastic sheet is used between the bricks and the retained soil it acts rather like the damp proof course of a house and keeps the bricks dry.
Barrett:	Is that expensive to do?
James:	Not really, but with bricks you will need some form of capping to stop the rain soaking in at the top.
Barrett:	Is this the stuff that has to be ordered specially?
James:	Oh no! This is readily available. No problems with that.

Pause

	Just a minute though, I've just remembered that one of the builders merchants is doing a special promotion on ornamental walling. I could probably pick up the ornamental bricks at a reduced price.
Barrett:	Oh dear! I was just beginning to get away from the idea of ornamental walling because of the cost. Now I'm back where I started. (He sighs.) I'm really quite

confused.

James: Well, Mr Barrett. It's not for me to tell you what you should have. I think it has to be a personal choice. After all you're the ones who will have to look out at the wall every day.

Barrett: I suppose you're right. I'll have to discuss it with my wife when she gets back from her sister's. It's a pity really, I was hoping to get things moving.

James: Never mind. It can't be helped. You do need to be certain in your own minds about something like this. Let me know when you have decided what you want and I'll come around and give you a quote.

They shook hands. James retreated down the garden path leaving Barrett standing alone staring glumly at the patch of raised garden, trying in his mind's eye to visualize it surrounded with a decorative wall.

OPPORTUNITIES TO CLOSE
SUGGESTED ANSWERS

In this case study there were several opportunities for Derek James to pick up a buying signal and by doing so, to move the interview in his favour by bringing it nearer to a close.
Did you spot any of them?

Opportunity 1

Barrett: I would really *prefer something a little more rustic*.

The nature of this buying signal was Barrett volunteering his personal *preference*. James might have responded something like this:

James: I have a few samples of rustic brick in my van. Shall we look at them?

Opportunity 2

Barrett: Oh dear! *I didn't really want to spend too much.* After all we don't live out in the garden do we?

The nature of the buying signal, which is in italics, is an *objection*. James might have responded something like this:

James: Yes, I quite understand. (Agreeing.) How much did you imagine spending on the wall then, Mr Barrett? (Asking a question.)

With this information in his possession it would be relatively easy for James to come up with a proposition that would fit Mr Barrett's pocket.

Opportunity 3

Barrett: Are these bricks *easy to get hold of*?

Nature of the buying signal, a *question*. James might have responded as follows:

James: I'm sure I can get hold of them easily. Is that what you would like me to do, Mr Barrett?

Opportunity 4

Barrett: We would like to *get things moving quickly*.

Nature of the buying signal, a *committing statement.* James might have responded as follows:

James: When exactly would you want the work to start then, Mr Barrett?

Opportunity 5

Barrett: Well, *getting back to the bricks idea.* Can anything be done to stop them absorbing water?.

> The nature of this buying signal, which is in italics, is a veiled *committing statement.* Instead of replying as he did, James might have tried:

James: Are you beginning to prefer the idea of using bricks then, Mr Barrett? (Checking it out.)

> With this information James could tailor the rest of the interview in the direction favoured by Barrett and thereby improve his chances of reaching a positive conclusion.

Barrett: Now I'm back where I started. (He sighs.) *I'm really quite confused.*

> The nature of this buying signal is disappointment (body language of a sigh) and the need for more information to dispel the confusion. Again the signal is in italics. Knowing this James could have tried a summary close:

James: Well let us try to weigh up the pros and cons of the two types of wall logically. Let's take the brick first, Mr Barrett. In its favour are (a) it's less expensive, (b) the materials are readily available, (c) your wife likes the idea of brick. The only drawback is the absorption factor, but that can be easily overcome. Now the ornamental bricks — well they certainly look nice but (a) they are more expensive and (b) there could be a delay with the capping. It seems as though brick wins. What do you think Mr Barrett?

> Whatever Barrett's reply, James is now much closer to reaching a satisfactory conclusion.

This case study is clearly not a very complex sales situation and yet even then the salesman missed at least six opportunities to move nearer to a close by not spotting the buying signals. Did you spot any other opportunities to close? If there were at least six opportunities to close in this relatively simple situation, just think how many more might arise in a longer or more complex sales interview! Interviews that will be more like the ones that you are likely to have with your prospective clients.